CHRISTIANS

CITY

CLOTHES AND JEWELLERY

ENTERTAINMENT

FARMING AND FOOD

(*Continued at back of book*)

First published 1958

Reprinted 1959
Reprinted 1961

HULTON EDUCATIONAL PUBLICATIONS LTD.

55/59, Saffron Hill, London, E.C.1
Printed in Great Britain by
Hills & Lacy Limited
Watford, Hertfordshire

ANCIENT
ROME

by

C. A. BURLAND

Illustrated by

YVONNE POULTON

HULTON EDUCATIONAL PUBLICATIONS

CONTENTS

7

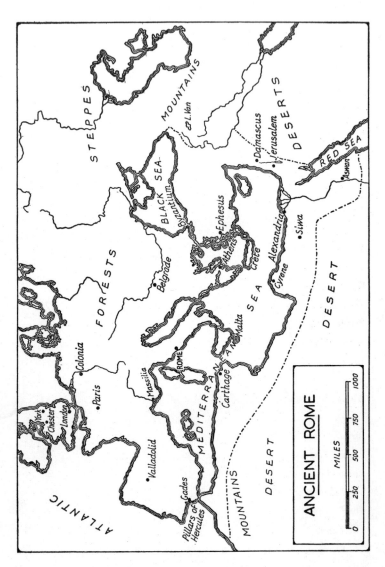

ANCIENT ROME

MILES

0   250   500   750   1000

City and Empire

Rome is the capital of Italy. It is now a beautiful modern city covering a group of hills beside the River Tiber, seventeen miles from where it enters the sea. You can find it easily on a map. The Tiber enters the Mediterranean Sea about half way up the western coast of Italy.

In ancient times Rome was the capital of a great Empire. The Romans ruled all the countries around the Mediterranean Sea, a great deal of central Europe and parts of western Asia. They also controlled France, England, Wales and parts of the lowlands of Scotland. Their greatest days were in the time of the Antonine Emperors, who reigned in the years about A.D. 150. In that time most of the great Empire was at peace, and most of the people in it ranked as Roman citizens. They did not think of themselves as Britons or Syrians or Spaniards or Egyptians, but they were Romans and very proud to bear so famous a name.

Roman Beginnings

Rome was founded in 753 B.C. by Romulus and Remus. The story tells us that they were twin brothers who were

The ancient bronze statue of the Capitoline Wolf

abandoned by their cruel parents and suckled by a she wolf on the Capitoline Hill. Later a shepherd found them and brought them up to lead a band of Latin tribesmen to build a little town of wood and clay huts on the hill above the River Tiber.

At first the Romans had to fight for life against attacks from other Latin tribes living near them; but they were led by wise Kings and gradually brought peace by conquering their enemies. The next struggle was with the Etruscan Kings who ruled all north Italy. The Romans at length defeated them and brought the whole of Italy under the rule of Rome.

By now the Kings had gone, and Rome was a Republic governed by a Senate. The Senators elected two Magistrates called Consuls, to lead the city and control the army.

How the Empire Began

The power of Rome aroused jealousies among the trading people of Carthage in North Africa. There were terrible wars in which the Carthaginians under their

The murder of Julius Cæsar

General Hannibal, threatened Rome by an attack through Spain and over the Alps. When the Romans had defeated Carthage they found that for safety they had to conquer Spain and a great part of North Africa.

Soon the Romans were involved in other wars, with Greece and the Greek cities of Asia. They were victorious, and Greece became a Roman Province.

Later on, the leaders of the Roman Senate quarrelled among themselves, and a tragic period of civil war began. Many people were killed and many cities burnt, but out of these struggles came the power of a great General, Caius Julius Cæsar. He invaded Britain in 55 B.C. He tried to make himself Dictator of the Roman Empire, but was murdered by people who stood for the old idea of a Republic.

The Cæsars

More wars followed, but finally Augustus Cæsar made himself master of the whole Empire. Officially he was only the leader of the Roman Magistrates, but in fact he was a dictator who ruled because he had absolute command of the Roman armies. Augustus was a wise and good man and the first of a long series of Roman Emperors. He it was who decreed that all the peoples of the Empire should be counted, and it was his order which sent Mary and Joseph travelling to Bethlehem on the first Christmas.

In the days after Augustus the chief dangers to Rome came from attacks by savage peoples on the borders of the Empire. The Emperors moved the limits of the Empire outwards to places where the country was more easily defended. In so doing they brought the Roman peace to tens of millions of people and helped them to live in a more peaceful and civilised way.

By the time of Antoninus Pius in A.D. 150, the Romans ruled an Empire more than a thousand miles wide and over two thousand miles long. If you look at the map you will see how it was protected by forests, rivers, and deserts on most of its borders. The army did not have many dangerously open frontiers to defend.

A Road to Rome

From all over the Empire roads led to Rome. If you were a Roman official in London you could reach Rome in five days. You would take a fast chariot over London Bridge, on to Canterbury and then to Rutupiæ (now Rye). Here you would board a fast rowing galley for Gessoriacum (Boulogne). On landing you would find

The road leading into Rome

another fast chariot waiting for you. The roads led across Gaul, first to Lutetia (Paris), and then across country to the Alps and into Italy. The road was called the via Flaminia and it led into Rome by the Flaminian gate.

The City of Rome

London and Paris were towns of importance in those days, but nowhere in the whole world was there any other place like Rome itself. Over two million people lived and worked in that great city. It spread over seven hills and down to the banks of the Tiber. Eight bridges led across the river to the suburbs.

The via Flaminia entered Rome from the north, through the Flaminian Gate. The road then went on to the great Baths of Agrippa, the beautiful Forum of Trajan, and to the base of the Capitol Hill where lay the sacred Forum Romanum. Here between the wonderful temples of marble and gold was the centre of the whole system of Roman roads, the Milestone made of solid gold and as tall as a tall man. The visitor would have

The Forum Romanun, the centre of the Empire

walked through the city to the Forum. Since the days of Julius Cæsar, nearly two centuries before, no wheeled traffic was allowed in the streets of Rome in daytime, except the great carts bringing building materials into the city.

A stranger visiting Rome for the first time must have been bewildered by the crowds, the noise and the great mass of buildings. Nowhere in the Provinces would one see a house of more than three stories, but here there were great blocks of tenement houses five and seven storeys high. In that age they seemed like sky-scrapers.

A Roman lady at home

Roman Homes

Life in the great city was quite different from life in the Roman Provinces. People were crowded together in blocks of flats, mostly one-room apartments. The wealthier people lived on the ground floor. They often had a little garden, and indoors a separate bedroom and kitchen. Their furniture was quite simple. There were tables, and couches on which they reclined when eating. Stools were used more than chairs and some were supplied with a low back, and arm rests. High-backed chairs were reserved for the Emperor and the great officers of the Empire. In the bedrooms there were single beds with no springs. They had mattresses stuffed with feathers or straw, and plain linen sheets. The rooms were lit only by little oil lamps.

Windows were either quite open, or covered up by slats of board which kept out rain and let in fresh air, but very little light. Palaces had windows of thin translucent sheets of alabaster. In a few places very great and rich people had

A Roman oil lamp

some glass in their windows, but it was not a clear transparent glass.

People who lived upstairs had to climb up narrow staircases set close to the walls of the rooms. In poorer tenements they went upstairs by ladder through a trapdoor in the floor. This was very different from the free life of a Roman villa in the countryside, but people put up with all the inconveniences because they loved the crowds and excitement of city life. Moreover all the best jobs were to be found in Rome if one only knew the right people.

A Morning in Rome

In the morning the Roman citizen would get up at sunrise. He had little to do but straighten his tunic, put on his sandals, and drink a glass of cold water. Then he would put on his cloak to go out. If he was a gentleman he first went to a reception room where he met his clients. These were people who did little jobs for him, and were always expected to praise him when they talked to others. They hoped that one day he would find them a good job in the government service. Meanwhile he gave them regular presents of money and food.

After an hour or so of these interviews he would go

off to make his toilet. The
public toilets were better than
anything in a Roman house
because they were all supplied
with fresh water and connec-
ted to the great sewers under
the city. At this time people
met to exchange the morning
news. There were no news-

Toilet implements

papers in ancient Rome. Afterwards the Roman might
visit the barbers to have his beard trimmed. If he were
young, or very vain he would be shaved. Very often the
best barbers were well-trained slaves. They used their
soft iron razors to scrape the skin of their masters. It was
quite painful because they had no ideas about shaving
soap, and only wetted the face with water before
beginning to scrape.

Having left the barber the Roman would wrap his
cloak about him and go on to his business. Maybe he
would visit the shops he owned and give orders to the
managers; or he might go to the courts to witness a
lawsuit in which he had an interest.

This would mean a short walk to the centre of the
city. In the courts there was always a great crowd of
people who enjoyed listening to the arguments of the
lawyers.

The Law Courts

The Romans prided themselves on their Law. It was very exact and very fair. It was the basis from which most of the laws of the European and American nations of today arose. If a man had a grievance, and the lower courts would not give him justice, he could appeal to the Emperor in person. It was unusual for a man to speak for himself in a lawsuit. He would employ one of the

A lawyer argues a case before the Magistrates

clever lawyers, who knew all the rules, to speak for him. These lawyers were specially trained in the schools. Their profession was thought to be the most important one a Roman could follow.

The law courts were great halls with a raised dais at one end where the magistrates were seated. Before them the case was argued by the lawyers, and witnesses were called to give evidence. There was no jury. The magistrates had to listen to all the arguments and try to reach a just decision themselves about the rights and wrongs of the case.

Because the Emperor was, by law, the first magistrate of Rome, he was bound to appear in the courts on most mornings. He spent a lot of his time listening to the cases being argued before him. It must often have seemed a waste of time for a very busy man, but to every citizen of the vast Roman Empire it showed that the Emperor himself was obedient to Roman Law.

At midday the Romans would go to a light meal at home, or else at one of the many shops where cakes and wine and hot snacks of various kinds might be bought.

The Public Baths

The afternoon was the time for a visit to the Thermæ,

The hall of one of the public Baths

or Baths. These buildings were enormous halls with walls and columns of fine marble, and rich decorations in mosaic work and painting. Most of them had been built for the people of Rome by the Emperors. For the equivalent of a penny in our money one could have all one desired of beautiful surroundings, warmth and health.

As soon as the Baths were opened the bathers streamed in. Friends met to talk, business men came to discuss trade, lawyers chatted over their new cases. Slaves came to look after their masters and to help them to dress elegantly. Poor men came to find comfort, and for an hour or two to live like the Emperor.

In the Baths clothes were left behind in the dressing rooms. Then one went into a big hall where the floor was warmed by hot air flowing from furnaces beneath the building. As soon as one felt ready one went into the Hot Room. It had a plunge bath of hot steaming water, and the floor was heated so much that it was uncomfortable to walk on for any length of time. Here the bathers perspired and scraped themselves clean. Their slaves or the bath attendants would massage them and oil their skins if they wished. After this came a dive into a cold plunge bath, to close the pores and tone up the skin. After this they dried and some were rubbed down with scented olive oil.

After the bath they would put on light clothes and go to the sports ground or games rooms to get some refreshing exercise. Or maybe they would look in the library and take down a roll of papyrus to read for a while. More often than not they would read aloud with a group of friends. Here they could meet friends in comfortable surroundings.

The Evening Meal

After the Baths the day was really over for the ordinary Roman. It was then time to go home to the crowded little flat, and prepare for dinner. On the way food would be bought, and at home the women of the household would do the cooking on little charcoal stoves. One had to be very careful in the overcrowded city because of the danger of fire. The stoves were usually kept on blocks of stone or sheets of metal.

The meal was taken at a low table surrounded by couches. On these the diners reclined at their ease and ate with the help of their fingers and table knives. Meat was often served ready cut up on wooden skewers; it

A small charcoal stove

was easier and cleaner that way. There were many kinds of green vegetables and root vegetables. Nettles were stewed, and eaten like spinach by the Romans. They had no potatoes, but there were carrots and parsnips. They had good bread too, mostly in round loaves. For drink there was usually wine mixed with water. The evening meal was quite a heavy one. It was the main meal of the day. The diners rinsed their fingers and mouths after eating. They then went off to their little bedchambers.

Rome at Night

Romans only took off sandals and outer garments for sleeping. Then they closed their windows, wrapped themselves under the coverlet and tried to sleep. It was well known that people did not enjoy much sleep in Rome. Carts were allowed into the city at night, and the narrow stone alleyways would rattle with the noise. Horses and carts would bring in new things for the shops. Slow heavy ox carts brought in foodstuffs from farms in the country. Maybe an official would try to drive through the throng in a chariot amid a noisy shouting from the carters who had to make way for him.

Often, too, there was the noise of running men carrying ladders and poles. These were the firemen running to some house where a little oil lamp had spilt, or a cooking stove upset to cause a fire. The fire brigade might make a bucket chain to bring water if they happened to be near the river or a fountain. In most cases all they could do was to hurry the people out of the burning buildings and pull away the timbers into the open street. Often enough a building had to be pulled down to prevent a fire from spreading. The city was burnt down once in the reign of Nero, who blamed it on the Christians. But it was only through constant action by the fire brigade with its primitive equipment, that Rome was not burnt down every few years.

There was also a danger of some big tenement block collapsing. The Romans were fine builders, but these houses were often built for cheapness, and the walls were only just strong enough to hold up the great weight of the upper storeys. A single broken beam of bad timber might start a collapse which could cause a number of deaths and leave a hundred people homeless. It was because of this danger that, during the day time, the only wheeled vehicles allowed in Rome were the carts of the builders.

Palaces and Gardens

Within the city there were many palaces, some belonging to the Cæsars and others to very rich landowners. These palaces were built of massive brickwork overlaid with marble, and decorated with gilded bronze. Inside many of the great halls the walls were painted with scenes of architecture and open air scenes; it gave the appearance of a view of the country or the seaside.

Indoors, and also in the fine gardens, there were statues of the ancestors of the family, and some of the gods and heroes of Roman history. They were all painted very carefully in life-like colours. Many of them had been taken from Greece, because the Romans thought that Greek art was better than their own.

Rich men were very proud of their interest in the arts. They collected statues and bronze figures, and employed

Talking about poetry in a palace garden

the best painters to decorate their houses. Landscape gardeners arranged the grounds as beautifully as possible on the hilly slopes of Rome. Often the owner would invite writers and poets to dine with him and his other guests, so that they could enjoy the newest works of literature.

But there were also people who had no care for art, and bought fine things just to be able to show how fashionable they were. They gave noisy parties with singers and dancers from the theatres and circus, and there was a great deal of drunkenness. But no one worried very much, because the Romans liked to enjoy themselves in a noisy way, and most of them preferred fine food and drinks to all the books in the world.

The Amphitheatre

On great occasions the people went to the amphitheatre. This was an excitement for them, of a kind which we should hate. Gladiators fought and killed each other there. They were mostly either slaves or desperate men who did not care much whether they lived or died. Some were given armour to wear, others fought with nets and tridents as if they were fishermen. Sometimes men were pitted against wild animals. Sometimes crimi-

The Emperor at the Games

nals were sent in unarmed to be killed by lions, elephants or bulls.

In between the events there were true circus performances. Trained elephants danced, acrobats did marvellous balancing tricks, and troupes of dancers made wonderful pattern dances for the pleasure of the people.

These games were given for the people of Rome by the Emperor, who was always present in his Royal Box. The people loved to feel that their Emperor was among them enjoying the games as much as they did themselves.

People who did not go to the games were looked on as silly. Sometimes they were suspected of being Christians. It was dangerous to be a Christian in those days; but no one who believed that men should live to love one another for God's sake would go to those terrible games of the ancient Romans.

Theatres and Artists

There were many theatres in Rome, but they did not always present plays. The great plays of the ancient Greeks did not suit the Romans. They preferred something more amusing. There were many musical plays about the adventures of the gods in their visits to the earth, often very funny and not very respectable. Other shows were much more like what we should call Variety, with performances by popular singers, dancers and acrobats. These were very skilled people and the Romans paid them highly. A singing star or famous dancer might rise to almost any heights in society. Such artistes were often guests of the Emperors.

Famous performers were sometimes honoured by a statue erected in a public place. But the reward they most coveted would be a gift of a house in the country made by the Emperor or a rich private citizen.

Nero

Nearly a hundred years before the time of Antoninus Pius poor crazy Nero used to sing and play on the lyre in the theatre, like any of the famous public performers. People were afraid to criticise that Emperor for fear that he would have them murdered.

A statuette of Nero

Apart from this Nero was remembered for the great fire of Rome, and the gigantic gilded statue of himself which used to stand in front of the Colosseum. The amphitheatre was named from the colossal statue. It was built by Vespasian, whose son Domitian hated Christians and had many of them murdered there. It used to seat fifty thousand people. Nero also built a Circus on Vatican Hill. It was here that he had St. Peter the Apostle crucified. But later on it was used only for its proper purpose of Chariot Racing.

Chariot Races

We can share the Roman love for chariot racing. It was a very fast, exciting game. The light chariots were pulled by teams of four horses. The course was seven times round the wall down the centre of the circus. This added up to about two and a half miles. There were usually four teams, the Reds, the Greens, the Whites and the Blues. The teams were lined up by the presiding magistrate, who was dressed like the Emperor in purple and gold. He threw a white cloth into the arena, and then the racing teams were off.

The exciting moments were the sharp turns at the end of the circus. Here the chariots would try to get to the inside of the curve, and just miss the wall as they swept round. If they were too near to each other there would be a spill as the wheels touched. The light chariot would fall apart and the wheels go spinning along among the frightened horses. The race attendants would dash up to drag the charioteer to safety before the other chariots came round on the next lap.

Charioteers wore crash helmets and padded body

armour, so they were rarely seriously injured. But the crowds were much too intent to worry about that. They were cheering their favourite colour on to victory, or betting on the results. It was a noisy happy scene. In the great Circus Maximus a quarter of a million people found places to watch the sport.

Successful charioteers soon became famous, and were honoured in every way just as famous sports stars might be treated in our days.

Baking Bread

Although Romans enjoyed themselves every afternoon with some spectacle or the Bath, the morning was a busy time for work.

Thousands of slaves toiled at the stone mills in the bakeries. Corn was poured into the top of a large mill-stone, through which a hole led it to the lower millstone. The slaves pushed the upper stone round and round by means of wooden bars set into it. As the corn was ground into flour it was run into baskets and taken over to wooden troughs. In these it was made up into round loaves and shovelled into an enormous brick oven, beneath which a fire of wood was kept blazing. As each batch of loaves rose and turned a nice crisp brown

33

c

1. Pouring in grain   2. Turning the mill   3. Kneading dough
4. Baking bread

outside, it was shovelled out and a new batch put in.

There were always people ready to collect the fresh loaves and take them to the food shops or sell them round the houses. They carried them in baskets on their backs.

Shops in Rome

The shops and market places of Rome were always

34

busy. Many people bought their food ready cooked at the shop-front taverns. Merchants sat among their goods in their dark, arched shops. They sold all manner of things: food, meat, knives and metal work, carpets from Persia, muslins from India, silks from China, furs and metals from Britain, corn from Tunisia, paper from Egypt, timber and amber from Germany, horses from the Danube, incense from Arabia, copper from Spain, silver from Greece.

In fact, in one or other of the shops in Rome one could find anything from the known world. There were

A cloth merchant's shop in Rome

35

even shops where one could buy magic and lucky charms, though nobody can tell us if they really worked.

Shopkeepers banded together in trade associations to make sure that they were not charged too much rent for their shops. But they could charge high prices to their customers. There were no big stores as we know them. It was rare for a shopkeeper to have more than two

The dangerous moment in a char

assistants in the business. He usually had a shop on the ground floor of a building and a storeroom in the basement. In some of the big markets, however, shops were on four or five floors, one above the other. In these the wine shops were mostly upstairs, and it must have been very dangerous to stagger out of them drunk. All the wine shops, called tabernæ (taverns), hung a bough

e, rounding the end of the course

with green leaves outside their doorways to show when they were open to serve customers.

Roman Artisans

The shops of the artisans were busy places. The potters would do some of their work in finishing off their wares in the shop. The cutlers would have a little charcoal furnace in which they could temper their knives and scissors, and a work bench where they could polish and sharpen them on fine hone stones.

They also sold razors, but they were not very clever in making really sharp ones. The jewellers also had small furnaces, for enamel work. They were always ready to fit a ring to a lady's finger, or add an extra link to her necklace, whether it was of fine gold or only polished brass. In other shops, where they sold glass ware, it was no unusual sight to see simple little scent bottles being blown out of bubbles of molten glass at the end of

Roman toilet articles for the ladies

an iron tube. When the little bottle was blown into shape
it was cooled by swinging it in the air, and then a quick
line, drawn with a diamond, would cut it off the stem.
These little shops of the Roman artisans must have been
fascinating places to visit.

Roman Women

The Roman ladies did a good deal of their own shop-
ping, or sent their slave girls to do it for them. They
were expected to know all about where to buy the best
things at the lowest prices, and where the latest fashions
in cloth were to be found; whether they wanted it for
their own clothes or for their menfolk. They were not
supposed to be so clever as men, but in fact a few of
them owned businesses. Some of them were writers as
well as housewives. Living in Rome was difficult, and
they did not like large families of children, mostly
because of the lack of space. But they were very kind to
children, and did not beat them. That was left until the
children went to school. The women did the cooking
and ate their meals beside their husbands. When they
went out they wrapped themselves up, and partly hid
their faces in the folds of their colourful headscarves.
They went to theatre and circus; they cheered the

gladiators in their fights, and clapped their hands and waved their headscarves to their favourites among the charioteers.

Girls in Rome

Girls did not go out much in Rome. They stayed at home, and their mothers taught them to read and write. They also learnt how to cook and do embroidery. If they were the daughters of a rich family they would have a governess, who was usually one of the family slaves, to teach them. They might find as they grew up that they had not much housework to do. Then they could take up sports like archery and gymnastics, or even win fame as young poetesses. Singing and dancing were thought of as jobs done by people who worked in the theatre, and not quite the things for young girls to learn.

Girls of the poorer families would learn a little reading and writing from their mothers. They also learned something of a trade in order to earn a little money to help keep them. Maybe they would learn to weave, or help in a shop for women's things. Some were waitresses and dancers in the taverns, some were trained for the theatre as singers, dancers and musicians. They were to be found working in the amphitheatres as

Girls beating out the washing beside the river

cleaners, and attendants. They also washed clothes by beating them thoroughly on rocks in the river. Sometimes they used a simple kind of soap of fat boiled with wood ashes; but most of the dirt was simply beaten and slapped out of the cloth on the wet rocks. But, of course, every girl's dream was to be married and live happily ever after. Most of them did that and grew up to be the respected mothers of Roman families.

Boys at School

Boys were usually sent to school. It was not a free

school. Every pupil had to bring a little money to help keep the teacher. They learned to read and write. In school reading was always done aloud. They used an alphabet like ours for writing, except that I was used for both I and J, and V used for both U and V. They learned to write on boards which were covered with a thin layer of wax. On the wax they wrote with a metal stylus, something like a knitting needle. When the writing was finished and done with, they could clean it all off by just warming the wax and smoothing it over the board ready for use another time.

Arithmetic was quite difficult, because they used letters for their numbers. I=1, II=2, V=5, but IV=1 less than 5=4, and VI=5+1=6. X=10, XXX=30. L=50, C=100, D=500 and M=1,000. Our number 1959 would have to be written with MCMLIX. That is one thousand, and one hundred less than a thousand, fifty and one less than ten. You will find it quite impossible to do any sums by just using the letters. The Roman boys used an abacus, which was a frame with beads strung in rows of tens. They calculated their arithmetic, just as the infants do simple sums on counting frames today. They became very quick at this, and wrote down the answer in capital letters.

History was simply a list of the Cæsars and of the events which happened in their reigns. To make it more

Boys reading and writing in school

complicated the Romans counted the years by names. Each year was named after the two consuls who were in charge of the city during that year. All dates were calculated from the foundation of Rome, so our year A.D. 150 was the year of Rome 903.

The great men of the past were the subjects of the important history lessons. From their stories the Roman boys learned how to be good Roman men. They wanted to be brave as Horatius who held a bridge single handed against an Etruscan army; or as cautious as the General Fabius who slowly led the Carthaginian armies into a trap.

43

In geography lessons they learned about the Empire. They had to know the names of cities, rivers and peoples, and where the great mountains, rivers and deserts marked the borders of their Empire. They knew what things were brought in trade from distant places. Their maps were quite good, but many were simply lists of towns, with a line running between them to show which roads led through them as they went from Rome to the boundaries of the Empire.

The Romans did not think that their Empire was the entire world. They had learned about India, whence came muslins, gold, peacocks and jewels; and about China whence the merchants brought beautiful silks. They knew of a land of black peoples south of the Sahara, and even heard about strange fur-clad men who looked like animals and lived in far north Lapland. They did not like foreign peoples. They thought of them as mere savages who were not wanted in the Empire unless they came as slaves or as mercenary soldiers.

Sports were not a school subject at all; but Roman boys practised running and jumping. They climbed and swam, and wrestled as all boys do.

The Roman love of law, and the speech making that went with it, made them give a special place to speech training in school. The bigger boys learnt a lot about grammar and poetry. Later they went on to learn the art of public speaking. It was important to know how to give expression to the voice; but equally one must know how to stand, and how to use arms and hands to emphasise the meaning of the words. It was even necessary to know the meaning of the positions of one's fingers when speaking.

Another problem for the Roman orator was how to manage his clothes. The toga worn by grown men on official occasions such as a visit to the Courts, was a heavy and difficult garment. Youngsters spent a lot of time learning to wear it properly, and hold it so that it fell in graceful folds over their arm when they were speaking. It would never do for a lawyer to keep on hitching up his clothes while making a speech.

Men's Clothing

Clothes were a problem for all Romans because they had to cope with a hot Italian summer and a cold wet winter. They had wool and linen to choose from. They began with a loin cloth rather like a baby's napkin. Over this the men wore a short tunic reaching to the knees, and sometimes another hip-length tunic over this. For normal occasions they wore a cloak, and in winter this was long and thick with a hood to protect the head.

45

Gentlemen and elderly men wore ankle-length tunics.

They preferred white clothes with simple embroidered borders. One could judge the rank and social position of a man of good family by the amount of tyrian purple on his clothes. The Emperor, of course, wore a purple robe. This Roman purple was a gorgeous deep red. Less important men had the purple on the borders of their robes, either in thick or thin lines according to their rank. Only the older and richer families were allowed to do this. The commoners had to wear either plain white, or sometimes a simple grey cloth.

A Roman man wearing his toga

Ladies' Fashions

Ladies were more magnificently attired. They had a wide freedom of colour and loved brilliant yellow and orange. Their underclothes were again a simple loin cloth, then came a long full gown hanging in folds down

A Roman lady in walking
dress

to the feet. For cold weather it would have sleeves. Over this they wore a long bright coloured tunic, and sometimes a shorter tunic of contrasting colour on top. There were many ornaments to the dress; big brooches were worn on the shoulder or sometimes on the chest; and a beautifully embroidered stole was worn around the neck hanging over the shoulders. A kind of handkerchief hung from the wrist. They wore headscarves to go out, and in winter they wore thick cloaks with hoods. Both men and women wore sandals, but they also had boots of soft leather, and women often wore pretty little shoes which covered the instep. These were decorated with coloured embroidery. For sports and games the women wore short tunics. Dancers had thin gowns and many scarves of different colours to wave gracefully as they danced.

47

Special Clothes

On great occasions ladies wore fine oriental silks and richly embroidered shawls. The men were obliged to wear their togas. These were semi-circular pieces of cloth five yards in diameter. They wrapped them round, with one end tucked into the waist after it had passed over the shoulder from behind. The other end was carried on the arm. It was a most dignified garment, and very beautiful when it hung properly; but it was heavy, and a terribly difficult thing to put on so that it looked just right.

Officers in the army also had a difficult dress. They wore the usual loin cloth, and a tunic with short sleeves and a full kilt. This was often red in colour. On top of this came an elaborate breast-plate with figures of gods and heroes all over it. It was made of brass and had to be highly polished. Then came a short kilt of thick leather. Their military boots had fine leather straps. On the left hip they hung the short thick sword in a decorated scabbard. When visiting they carried their fine brass helmets under their arms. On parade they wore the helmet, and it looked very brave with its crest bristling on top. Some great officials had parade helmets with a complete mask of polished brass covering their faces so that they must have shone brilliantly in the sun.

The Army

There were too many Roman citizens for all the men to be in the army. The Legions which made up the army varied in numbers from two to ten thousand men. These came under four army commands guarding the frontiers. The Legions were not normally stationed in the interior of the Empire.

A soldier of the Guard

A very special body of soldiers, the Prætorians, who were the personal guards of the Emperor, were stationed in Rome itself. They were bigger, smarter, and more splendid than other soldiers. The Prætorians were often involved in plots to overthrow one Emperor and make a new one, but in the time of

49

D

the Emperor Antoninus Pius they were contented and well paid.

Most soldiers joined the Roman army for the sake of earning a living, and for the interest of the travel which it afforded. They were never well paid, and part of their wages was given in bars of salt. Their uniform was a loin cloth, thick tunic, leather jerkin, iron breast-plates and iron or bronze helmet. They had thick leather sandals held by strong straps which also acted as a protection to their legs. Packs were carried on their backs, and these included a short spade which could be used for throwing up a defensive earthwork quickly if they had to camp in hostile territory at night. Usually there were wagons to carry the heavy baggage, but if necessary a soldier was expected to carry up to eighty pounds of equipment with him. A day's march was between twenty and thirty miles, according to the kind of country. About forty days marching would take one from Rome to Britain. Army life was not hard. Within the Empire soldiers would find good quarters and food ready for them, and on the frontiers there were great fortified camps well organised for the exactly regulated life in the army.

The army came quickly into action when the tribes across the frontiers made a raid. The smoke of a burning village, or the arrival of a messenger calling for help, would be a signal for the cavalry to set out. If the party of raiders was small, the cavalry would charge them and drive them back over the borders. Such small bands of wild raiders could not stand up to the organised Roman troops. Their spears, thrown from a distance, were warded off easily, and it was impossible for them to escape the thrust of a Roman sword at close quarters.

A big organised raid by the warriors of a whole tribe was a different matter. The cavalry then became scouts, reporting on the movement of the enemy, while a legion of foot soldiers would march to some point at which

Soldiers in battle

they could force the raiders to come to battle. If time permitted they would camp and throw up an earthwork which would protect their stores, and perhaps tempt the enemy to attack a fortified position where he was sure to be beaten back. But more often they would have to attack the barbarians at once.

After a volley of heavy throwing spears had opened the way, the Roman soldiers marched shield to shield, pushing their way into the enemy, stabbing and cutting with their short swords. If one man in the front line fell, another would step in to replace him. This organised force would break up most opposition. As soon as the enemy were busy fighting the legionaries, there would be charges on their flanks by the cavalry until the raiders broke up and fled back to their forests.

Military Roads

Roman soldiers were much more than simple fighting men. They had to build bridges and roads, and even to make stone buildings. Among them were metal workers to repair armour, and swordsmiths to keep the weapons in order. Highly skilled army engineers often accomplished difficult work. Along a rocky stretch of the Danube they managed to cut holes in sheer cliffs overhanging the river. In these holes they fitted beams of timber, and along the beams they laid a roadway of planks. A guard rail was fitted at the edge of the road over the river. Like most Roman roads this was made so that the army could move quickly from place to place.

Roman roads were usually made for the army. They kept to a standard width of about fifteen feet. In some places they were built with stone blocks, in others they were made of rammed gravel and sand. On swampy ground they were built on piles.

When a road was being built the army surveyors went

Surveyors planning a new road

ahead and planned the route. As far as possible roads were made straight. A bend in the road meant more paces for the soldiers marching along it. Bends were more usual in hilly country where it would have been too hard to march straight up the steep slopes. The surveyors knew the general direction in which their road must run. They would find some point on the sky-line to aim for. It might be a hill top, or a tree, or the smoke of a fire lit by men sent on ahead to make a marker beacon.

Building a Road

Roman surveyors used an instrument called a groma. It was a pole with two cross pieces at the top. On two ends of the cross pieces they hung weighted strings. Then they turned the pole so that the two strings were in line with the eye and also in line with a sighting point on the horizon. As the workmen went forward marking the line which the road was to take, the surveyors signalled to them to move to right or left, so that the road should always be in line between the strings on the groma and the distant sighting point.

The next step was to dig a trench on each side of the road. This would drain off water and keep the track dry.

The turf was trimmed off and piled on the far side of the ditches. Then the track was dug down to gravel or sand and levelled. On top of this a layer of bigger stones was rammed well in. It was smoothed over by a wash of muddy lime and sand which bound the stones together like mortar. Such a road needed a good deal of care to repair it every Spring, but, if it was well drained, it kept fit for use for centuries.

How a Roman road was made

Sometimes it was necessary to take the road through a swampy patch of ground. Then the great beams of oak or elm, which would not rot in wet soil, were hammered down until they reached firm ground, beneath the swamp. On these, beams made from sections of tree trunks were laid, and the spaces between were filled with smaller timber. Such places on the roads were always bumpy, but they were safe and saved miles for the traveller.

Among mountains, however, Roman roads could not run straight but kept to the valleys and easier slopes.

Trade and Roads

Every town had to keep its sections of road in good repair. People had a lot to gain by good roads, which brought traders from all parts of the Empire. We know of a Syrian trader buried at York, where he must have died on a business journey. There was once a Roman mission to China, where traders were already doing business for spices and silks. From Rome to the edge of

Roman Ambassadors visit the Emperor of China

the deserts the road was the Roman Imperial road. Across the deserts there were caravan trails leading to the mountains, and then the Roman visitors came to another Empire and new roads leading to the great cities of the Han Emperors of China. Other caravan roads went from the deserts through Persia to Baluchistan and to India. From Arabia and India trading ships went on voyages to the rich spice islands of Indonesia.

Except in China and India there were no roads beyond the frontiers of Rome. Trackways for men and bullock wagons led through the great forests of Germany. Further east the horsemen of the steppes needed no roads.

In the reign of Antoninus Pius there was only one area where the frontiers of the Empire needed to be moved, and that was Scotland. Here the Caledonian tribes had taken to raiding the rich towns of Britain, so the army was called out to build a new fortification and roads between the Firths of Forth and Clyde. This line was not held for long, and soon the defences of Britain were withdrawn to Hadrian's Wall further south, much of which still stands today.

The Post

Within the Empire there was peace, and free movement

of people and trade. The roads were Imperial Ways, used by troops and the Imperial Post. This was for the service of the Emperor. The public had to arrange for the transport of their own letters. For the Emperor there were fast chariots which conveyed documents from one post house to another, with a change of horses every few miles. This post could travel about two hundred miles in a day to any part of the Empire. It was the means by which the Emperor and his officials knew what was going on in every part of the enormous area which they ruled. Ordinary citizens often sent letters to their friends by merchants who were travelling quickly with perishable goods. Their letters were written on wax-lined tablets of wood. The people who received them read the letter. Then they smoothed the wax and sent back the reply, written on the same wooden tablet.

The Roman Navy

On the seas there were ships. Some were small, fast rowing galleys. Other bigger ones for war, were made with a kind of castle fore and aft from which soldiers could hurl heavy stones to sink the enemy. Warships were also equipped with rams at the water line so that they could be rowed against the enemy ships to sink

A big merchant ship under sail

them. The biggest ships were merchantmen. They sometimes carried more than one mast, and relied on sails as much as on their row of oars. They were often over a hundred feet long and carried great cargoes of grain, timber and wine. Independent sea rovers went off on pirate raids and stole and murdered even in the Mediterranean Sea, but the Roman navy was always on patrol and if a pirate fleet was encountered, there would be a battle. Usually the pirates were defeated and those who were captured were either nailed up on crosses beside

59

the roads, to die slowly as a warning to other people, or they were bundled off to be killed in the amphitheatres by gladiators or wild beasts for the pleasure of the citizens.

Punishment of Criminals

Criminals were brutally treated in Roman times. The law was just and clear and the Romans prided themselves upon it. Civil law dealt with money and land and could be settled by payments and fines; but crimes such as robbery, violence, contempt of the Emperor, and insults to the gods were punished by cruel force. A debtor might be sold into slavery, or thrown into prison, but real criminals had little hope of life. The scourging of a criminal was done with leather whips with pieces of lead tied at the ends. People suspected of knowledge of crimes were brought to prison and tortured until they said whatever was wanted of them.

It was the usual thing for thieves and lesser criminals to be nailed up on crosses, to be laughed at until they died after two or three days. The more famous criminals were reserved for the amphitheatre and killed there. Even a humane Emperor like Antoninus Pius could not control the strange savagery of the Roman citizens.

The cruel punishment of death on a cross

They wanted their brutal games, and the Emperor was bound to provide them for fear of being overthrown himself by a popular uprising. The games had started long ago as a special sacrifice for the spirits of the ancestors, and the people always felt that they were a part of the Roman religion.

The Roman Religion

The official Roman religion was rather like the Greek one. There was a father of the gods, Jupiter The Thunderer, his wife Juno, and a group of other gods and

61

A marble head of Jupiter

goddesses; Venus the goddess of love and her son Cupid; Vulcan lord of fires; Mercury the messenger of the gods, and Mars the god of battle. There were also family gods, the Lares and the Penates who looked after the affairs of the household. The great gods were worshipped in magnificent temples, and their images were to be found in many places with altars in front of them, so that people could make offerings. The Spirit of Rome was also a goddess, and the Romans worshipped the divine power of the Emperor.

The official religion was a matter of politeness and good order to most Romans. It helped them to honour their ancestors and to obey the laws of their beloved city and respected Emperor.

This religion had very little personal appeal to the intelligent Romans. They saw that it was just one of many religions in their great Empire. Many of them also followed other religions which promised them some

62

kind of personal salvation from the troubles of this life. The favourites among these cults were those of the Persian sun god Mithras, and the Egyptian goddess Isis. Their secret ceremonies led people who went through them to believe that they were given peace of soul and freedom of mind from the evils of the world around them. These religions spread rapidly over the Empire. They allowed soldiers and citizens to follow the official religion and make offerings to Mars, and the Spirit of Rome and the Emperor.

Persecution of Christians

The Romans usually adopted other people's gods when they took over their countries. They gave them names which fitted them into the official Roman religion, and then told the people that they must also make offerings to the Spirit of Rome and the Emperor. Only two groups of people would not fit in, the Jews and the Christians. They both believed in God, one God, who would not allow them to worship any other gods. It seemed strange to the Romans, as if these people hated the good fortune of Rome and the Emperor and would not wish them well. So it was not really surprising that most Roman officials did not try to understand Christianity. They hunted down the Christians as if they were enemies. The Emperor Antoninus Pius was not greatly interested in hunting down Christians. He preferred to spend his time doing the hard job of keeping his Empire well governed. Already there must have been thousands of Christians in the Empire, many of them living in Rome itself. They kept away from the games, did not go to the theatres and lived quietly. As far as possible they were never present when there was a ceremony at which incense was offered to the Roman gods or to the Emperor.

Early Christians in Rome

Roman law allowed people to form Burial Societies, which bought ground for cemeteries. Their members met from time to time to remember the dead and pray for them. The Christians registered themselves as Burial Societies. Then, on every seventh day, there would be a little meeting in one of the burial grounds. Some were held underground in the narrow passages of the catacombs, where a priest would silently offer the sacrament over the tomb of someone who had been killed for the sake of religion. Sometimes there was a quiet meeting and ''breaking of bread'' in one of the cemeteries.

There was one in particular to which Christian people came from all parts of the Empire. It was a little above-ground building, rather like a Roman temple, decorated with designs in plaster. It stood in the cemetery beside Nero's circus on Vatican Hill. Under it was the tomb where lay the remains of St. Peter the Apostle. To ordinary Romans there was nothing much in these quiet meetings, and they did not worry about them. The Christians kept their mouths shut and lived as a secret society. They had their secret ceremony of Baptism for joining the Church, and they came to communion

The little burial chapel on Vatican Hill

E

together. Among themselves they circulated the gospels and books written by their more famous teachers. A few were priests and the whole group of "churches" around a great city were ruled by a bishop. In Rome at this time the Bishop was named Pius. All the Christians looked up to him, because he was the head of their religion in the great city which was the heart of the Empire. He was the ninth successor of St. Peter the Apostle. In the year A.D. 157 he was arrested and ordered to worship the Spirit of Rome. He absolutely refused to do this, so he was killed. After him Anacletus was chosen by the Christians as their leader. It was to be another hundred and fifty years before a Christian became Emperor of Rome. Then, at last, the Church won freedom.

Roman Burials and Ancestor Worship

Although the Christians tried to bury their dead it was the Roman custom to cremate dead bodies. They kept the ashes of members of the family, arranged in special little urns, in a tomb for all the family. They thought the souls of their dead went to the underworld. Every year they honoured their ancestors by pouring out little offerings of wine before their statues which they kept in the house. It was for this reason that the Romans took so much trouble with portrait sculpture. If one's statue was going to be the centre of a family ceremony long after one had died, it was a good thing to have it carved so that it was a true likeness.

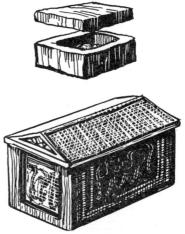

Stone boxes for the ashes of Roman dead

These busts and statues were painted to appear exactly like life, even to the coloured lines in the iris of the eyes. The same was done to all the statues of Emperors and gods which we now see only in the white marble. The Romans would laugh at us and think we only knew them as white-faced ghosts.

Roman Buildings

Romans loved good workmanship, and in particular they enjoyed fine buildings. The temples, palaces, and public buildings of Rome were magnificent and huge.

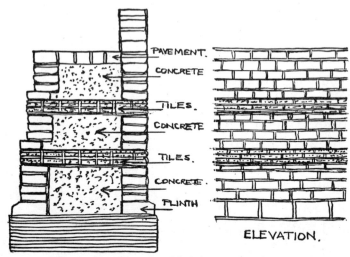

A Roman wall made of brick, stone and concrete

Where we would erect a big building of many small rooms, the Romans liked a few enormous halls richly decorated. Probably they felt the need for a change from the overcrowded small rooms in their city tenement houses.

The main walls of most of the great buildings were made of brick. The Roman brick was really a hard-baked red tile about 22 inches square and an inch and a quarter thick. These were made in half bricks and quarter bricks if they were needed. They were laid on foundations of fine cement mixed with powdered tiles, which made it pink in colour. Such walls of tiles and cement were very strong and would last for centuries.

Cement was obtained fairly easily near Rome. Limestone was burnt with great piles of timber in parts of the quarry where there was a steady draught of air. The powder of burnt lime was mixed with sand, ground-up tiles, and water to make cement. They could even make a kind of cement which would harden under salt water. They used this for building harbours.

Roman builders could cover the tops of doorways and windows by the use of great beams of wood or stone just as the Greeks did. Sometimes for big spans the Romans used beams of brass. They knew that brass was less likely to break than cast iron, and they had no steel for anything much bigger than a sword. But when they wanted to cover a really big space they used an arch of stone.

Building Arches and Domes

Roman builders were the first people to make full use of the arch. How they discovered the idea we do not know. It is not at all simple. One cannot throw an arch over a space without very careful preparation. First a scaffolding of wood was made, with boards laid from one side to another in an exact semi-circle. The Romans always used a semi-circular arch. Stones were then cut so that

Arches and how they
were made

they would fit into one another all the way round the curve. Front and back were straight, but the bottom of the stone had to be narrower than the top, and the sides sloping a little so that they should fit quite exactly against the next stones in the row. You will see that if any stone was left out of the arch it would fall down. The top stone of all was called the key-stone because it keyed all the other stones together. If any weight pressed on top of the key-stone the stone could not fall down because it was pressing firmly against the stones on either side of it and had no room to slip between them. One could go on putting weight upon an arch until the stone crumbled, or the walls at the side of the arch were pushed over.

If a row of arches were built one against another there would be a stone vault over a building, of the kind we call a barrel vault. One could use the same idea as the arch to build up a dome of many rings of shaped stone. The biggest dome the ancient Romans made is 142 feet across. It is the Pantheon of Marcus Agrippa which has now been standing since 27 B.C. This shows how strong a well-built dome can be.

Water Supplies

The arch was useful for many other things in addition to making roofs for buildings. Roman engineers knew

Rows of arches carrying a water supply across a river

how to make arches across a river to support a road bridge. They built great rows of arches across low country to carry aqueducts which brought water from springs in the hills into the cities.

In Rome there were a number of these aqueducts which brought fresh water to public fountains in the city. Very few people were rich enough to arrange for a supply of water to be brought directly into their houses. Mostly it was collected from the fountains by slaves. They carried pitchers of pottery, or goat skins, filled with water for use in the houses. Indoors it was kept in skins or large earthenware jars. The water for the great public baths came directly from the aqueducts. There was also a free-flowing supply for the public lavatories, which also kept the great sewers under the city clean and clear.

Country Villas

In the summer Rome was uncomfortably hot. Everyone who could moved out to a country house, or a pleasant villa at the seaside. The country houses and villas were quite unlike the great tenement blocks of the city. They were rarely more than two stories in height, and were built around a garden courtyard.

A Roman country house

Such houses were very pleasant places in which to live. One entered from the road through an archway into a little courtyard with a pool of rainwater in the centre open to the sky. Sometimes it was arranged that water from a nearby stream would make a small fountain. The path around the pool was covered by a tiled roof supported on columns. On one side there were sleeping rooms, and on the other the rooms for the domestic slaves. At the back was a spacious living room with painted walls, and simple elegant furniture. Sometimes

73

above the main hall there were one or two extra bed-rooms with windows commanding a view over the countryside.

Near Rome such houses were usually built away from the farm houses on the estates. But in the provinces such as Britain, the country villa was often the farm house as well. The back of the house looked out on the barns of grain and the stalls of the animals clustered around the farm yard. Also, in the provinces where the weather was colder than in Italy, it was usual to heat the floor of the main room, as well as the bath house, by hot air which flowed under them from a furnace at one side of the house. The hot air escaped through hollow tile flues within the walls of the rooms and so heated the whole house evenly. In Rome this was used in the great Baths, but not in private houses for fear of fire in the crowded city. In warmer parts of the Empire it was used only for

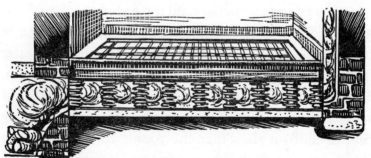

Roman central heating. The hot air from the furnace goes under the floor and through channels in the wall

the bath house. No Roman would think a country house was complete without its bath, consisting of a hot room and a cold plunge bath.

Roman Farms

Roman farmers were sometimes slaves, but there were a number of peasant farmers who were free. They worked very hard and had no machinery to help them. The fields were cultivated by a wooden plough with an iron share to turn the clods. It was usually drawn by a pair of bullocks. Many crops were grown: wheat, peas, beans, lentils, spinach, parsnips, cultivated nettles, carrots and turnips. There were all kinds of fruit trees, and usually a vineyard in the farm lands. Pastures were kept free for cattle, and on the hills there were many sheep and goats.

The farm people usually lived in small houses around the farm yards, near to their heavy work. Grain was reaped by hand, and all the threshing was done with wooden flails on a threshing floor. Planting and digging were all hand work with the spade. They knew a good deal about trees and looked after the timber on the estates. Wood of good quality always fetched a high price in Rome. It was carefully seasoned and then cut

A Roman farmer on his way to market

up by hand saws for use as building timber, or perhaps for use in ship building.

The Roman land owners had a great deal of their food sent in from their own farms. They were very proud of the care with which they managed the estates. But there was never enough food grown in Italy to keep the enormous population of the cities well fed. Food prices were always rather high and the farmers earned a good living for their work.

Trade in the Empire

The main granaries of Rome were North Africa and

Egypt, where great cornfields ripened rapidly under the tropic sun and more than one crop each year was possible. The Romans had to build enormous warehouses at the port of Ostia, to hold the great quantity of grain which came in from Africa. Roman energy and hard work encouraged the people of North Africa to keep the irrigation canals open, so that the land was always well watered and fertile.

From other parts of the Empire came other crops; dates and tropical fruits from the Near East, olives from Spain and Greece, and oranges from the Balearic Islands.

There was a great trade in metals. Silver came from Greece, copper from Cyprus, tin and lead from Britain, more copper and silver from Spain, gold from Egypt. Many jewels were brought by traders who came from India and Persia. Much trade was done through slaves, but a great deal of money was involved.

Roman Coins

The Romans used money far more than any other people of the ancient world. They made it of iron, copper, brass, silver and gold. Except for silver and gold the money was worth more than its value in metal.

The front and
back of a Roman
coin

Everyone accepted it in exchange for goods of about the
same value in any part of the Empire. Money was not
all minted in Rome itself.

Because of the danger of raids by bandits who might
seize a money wagon on a long journey, many provin-
cial mints issued coins for their Provinces in the name of
the Emperor.

Nearly all the coins were struck by hammering hot
metal on an anvil. A die carved in hard steel with the
design of the Emperor's head was laid on the top of the
blank, which was already lying on another die. This had
a design of Rome, Victory, or some other symbol carved
on it. A heavy blow with the hammer forced the heated
metal blank into the shape of the dies.

Roman Machines

The Romans had some idea of the use of natural power.
They made use of water wheels to lift water to irrigation

ditches. Water wheels were also used for working heavy trip-hammers by metal smiths. Sometimes they were apparently used for working mills. But on the whole Rome depended on human muscle power for her needs. Cranes, which were strong enough to lift heavy stones and beams of timber to the tops of the Roman palaces, were worked by slaves who stood inside a cage-like wheel with rungs on it. They climbed up on these rungs, and then their weight pulled the wheel round until they were at the bottom once again. So, always climbing and never going up, they kept the wheel-cage turning and so supplied the power to the great machine.

Using Pulleys

The Roman builders knew all there was to know about using pulleys to lift weights more easily. If they wanted to cut down by half the work of lifting a building stone, they would use two pulleys. First they tied one end of a long rope to a beam on the building a little above the height to which the weight was to be lifted. The rope was then brought down and passed through a pulley tied to the top of the stone. It was then run up again to another pulley on top of a wooden tower in front of the building. The pulley here was just at the same height as the end of

Lifting a building stone with the help of a pulley

the rope tied to the building. Next the rope came down from the tower to a team of labourers on the road. These men pulled the rope. For every yard of rope they pulled in, the stone was lifted half a yard. And so slowly and steadily they could haul it up until the masons on the building could pull the stone in and set it in position. Sometimes they used much more complicated arrangements of pulleys, but the principle was really the same. By making a weight move more slowly they were able to move it more easily.

Slaves

It was quite possible for the Romans to have made machines as we know them, but the idea never came to them. They had no need to invent such things because slaves did most of the heavy work.

Although the Romans owned slaves in great numbers, they were never quite sure whether slavery was a good thing or not. They accepted the need for slaves to do heavy work, and often enough they treated them cruelly. But they encouraged slaves to earn a little money and if possible to buy their freedom. On special occasions Roman gentlemen liked to set some of their slaves free. No head of a family would consider himself fit to die unless he had prepared his will and included the gift of freedom to some of his slaves.

The Romans were quite ready to see that a slave was a fellow human being.

Books and Libraries

The whole of the great Empire was run by Roman law. The Roman language, Latin, was used for all official documents, but in Greece and the Middle Eastern

F

A Roman public library. Nearly all the books are on scrolls

countries Greek was used as an equal language with Latin. Although many Romans enjoyed reading Greek books they thought that the Greeks were too clever with words to be of any practical value in the world. Nevertheless the Romans built fine public libraries which held books in both languages in every city of the Empire.

Most people could read and write a little, and nearly all could understand the books they borrowed from the libraries. Most of the books were written on long scrolls of Egyptian papyrus; but the book in the shape we know was becoming more popular all through Roman times. It began among the Greeks who sometimes bound up sheets of parchment like a book. Later on the Christians in Egypt made books of paper. They contained the Gospels and other teachings of the heads of the Church. If one was hunted down by the officials a little book was much easier to hide than a whole roll of papyrus.

Books for the libraries were written by scribes. These were usually slaves who worked with pen and ink at their desks in a scriptorium. At one end sat the reader

Copying out books in a scriptorium

slowly dictating the book, and below him sat a hundred or more men copying the words on to new paper sheets. They used a clear rapid handwriting, rather like our italic script. By this means the great libraries of the Roman Empire were kept supplied. In one of them, at Alexandria in Egypt, there were over two million books.

Latin Poetry

The Romans were interested in books, but they were specially attracted by poetry. They enjoyed the rhythm of words and loved a clever phrase. Famous poets were looked upon with the greatest respect, and their work was carefully studied in the schools, and imitated by grown-up writers. Among the greatest were Horace, Ovid and Terence. Their work was so good that it is studied today, and translations printed in English sell to millions of modern readers.

Latin was a particularly fine language for speaking aloud, the poets and writers of Rome made it very rich and expressive. In the immense Empire there were many dialects of Latin, but everywhere there were plenty of people who could read the poems of the famous writers aloud. Even in Britain such works were quoted in public and copied for the libraries.

Roman Artists

Just as the Romans loved elegant speech, so they liked elegance in their painting and decorative art. Apart from the realistic portraits of their ancestors they did not make many great works of art. They preferred prettiness and romantic subjects. Their favourite ornaments were garlands of flowers and dancing girls.

Inside their houses fresco paintings were made on the walls. This means that they painted on the plaster while it was still wet. The artist had his water paints ready mixed, sometimes with white-of-egg added to them to hold them more securely to the wall. He had to work quickly with a soft brush. Such artists could paint lovely portraits, landscapes, imitation columns and pretty gar-

The painted ceiling of a Roman palace

lands of flowers. They did all this in full colour and rich light and shade. They were so good that they must have practised their art until they could paint almost without having to think what they were doing.

Other artists modelled wall and ceiling decorations in plaster. Their plaster was made of burnt shell, or burnt gypsum rock, mixed with water. Plaster was strengthened by fibre added to the inner layers of the work, before the surface layer was put on.

They often made decorations of flowers and figures in moulds, and pressed them into the ceiling and wall plaster while it was still wet. Other workmen could mould the plaster into delicate shapes while it was moist.

Roman Pottery

The same kind of pretty poetic decoration was used on a great deal of Roman pottery. This was often made by pressing the clay into moulds while it was damp. The mould was then spun round on a turntable and the clay smoothed inside. As it dried it shrunk a little and could then be taken out of the mould without damage. The potters would then bake it in a kiln, which was very much like the kilns the Greeks used.

In different parts of the Roman Empire different

kinds of pottery were made. In the Middle East they fired a greyish yellow kind of pottery which was often left with a rough porous surface. In those hot lands water kept cool by gently evaporating through a porous pot. Some of the potters knew how to cover their pottery with a glaze. They crushed lead ore of the kind called galena and mixed it with fine silica sand. They painted this on the pottery with a little copper oxide mixed in it. When a pot painted with this mixture was put back in the kiln and heated up again, the lead and sand united to form a kind of glass which was coloured green by the copper. It made the pots look ornamental, and they would hold water without difficulty. If one kept fruit juice or wine in a pot lined with such a lead glaze it was dangerous to drink from it, because the acid in the drink dissolved some of the lead. One might die from the colic pains of lead poisoning.

In Britain some of the native potters at Caistor near Northampton made little bowls and vases in a smooth black pottery. On them they made lovely decorations in white clay, which was squirted on like sugar icing, from a little bag of leather. One of them was recently found near the valley of the River Neckar which formed the Roman frontier across Southern Germany. It must have been carried there by a soldier who had served in Britain.

Roman
pottery from
Britain

Red "Samian wares" were made in many parts of the
Empire, particularly in Gaul, as France was then called.
These were made in a clay which fired red. They were
finished by dipping in a very fine slip of liquid clay,
and burnt in the kiln to a smooth red which could be
burnished until it was quite shiny.

Roman Glass

The Romans were very good glass makers. Their glass is
always very light, and it was usually made from borax or
soda with silica sand and potash, though some heavier
and bluer lead glasses were made of a mixture more like
the potter's glaze. Some of the glass was melted in a
furnace and taken out on the end of a hollow iron or
bronze rod. The glass blower then spun his rod round
and blew through it until he had made the soft, hot glass

into the shape he wanted. At other times he would put the glass and rod into a fire-clay mould and blow until the glass was forced to fit into every corner of the mould before it cooled down and became solid. He knew how to run ribbons of softened glass on to hot glass vessels to make attractive ornaments. He could

The Portland vase

also mix glasses of different colours so as to twist them into coloured designs. One of the cleverest pieces of Roman glass work is the Portland vase. It was made of rich, dark blue glass which had been covered with a coat of white glass. The artists then polished away parts of the white glass so as to leave white figures and trees softly standing out on a dark blue background. It is a very beautiful as well as a clever piece of work.

The Emperor

The finest works of art went to the homes of the very rich and powerful among the citizens. Of course, the most gorgeous things were to be found in the Imperial Palaces. There were hangings of silk velvets imported from the East, canopies of cloth of gold, statues in ivory and marble, beautiful Greek bronzes, and small figures of solid gold. The dishes at an Imperial banquet were of gold and silver.

The Emperor himself was among the most magnificent beings in his Palace. His purple robes glowed a rich blood red above his golden sandals. His head-dress might be of linen or gold, perhaps a victor's crown of golden leaves might adorn his dark curly hair. Above him two great fans of ostrich feathers mounted on gilded poles were carried. When he rode through the city on his horse with its trappings of red leather and gold, the people would cheer and bow before him. If they crowded too near, the white-robed lictors pushed them back with bundles of rods around an axe. These signified the right of the Chief Magistrate of

The Emperor Antoninus Pius

Rome to deal out punishment, or even death, as the laws permitted. The Cæsar was never above the law, but most Romans would act as if he were, in himself, the only lawgiver.

In the Palace the Emperor was surrounded by his servants and ministers of state. Some of the greatest of these ministers were experts in special branches of government, such as Finance, Trade, or Road Services. Often these men had been born in the service of the Emperor as his slaves. As they learned, and became more important to him, he would give them the gift of freedom. Many Romans envied and hated these freedmen, but the Emperor knew well that because he had given them freedom they would be faithful and true to him; much more than members of many Roman families who prided themselves on being better born and more truly aristocratic than even the Emperor.

The Emperor as High Priest

The most important office held by the Emperor was *Pontifex Maximus*, which means High Priest. He it was who made the sacrifices of sheep and oxen to the great Jupiter in the ancient temple on Capitol Hill. He was both Priest and Emperor of the city and represented both the law and religion of Rome. For his priestly duties he wore white garments and a high crown made of golden bars and lined with white cloth. He recited the prayers to Jupiter, offered incense and supervised the killing and burning of the bodies of the sacrificed animals. On special occasions, when the offerings were made for divine help in some great enterprise, there were Augurs at the scene of sacrifice who solemnly read

The Emperor opens the gates of war

signs of success or failure from the shape and colour of the liver of a sacrificed pig.

When war was to be declared the Priest-Emperor solemnly went to the temple of the god Janus, and opened the gateways. The gates were only shut in time of peace, and that was very rare in Roman history. This temple of the two-faced god remained closed more often in the reign of Antoninus Pius than at any other time.

The Popes

At this time there lived the other Pius, the Bishop of the quiet Christians in Rome. On the Thursday before Easter he would wash the feet of the priests under him, as Jesus had done over a hundred and twenty years before in Jerusalem. His title was Bishop, but he liked to be known as the Servant of the Servants of God.

Nowadays we know of the ancient Emperors as wonderful people of long ago, whose Empire is gone and whose names are memories in history books. But today there is still a Bishop of Rome, the Pope, who is the head of the Roman Catholic Church. His Cathedral of Saint Peter covers part of the ruins of the Circus of Nero and the little temple above the burial place of Saint Peter.

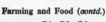